DOES THE BILL OF RIGHTS GIVE ME FREEDOM?

Government Book for Kids
Children's Government Books

Speedy Publishing LLC
40 E. Main St. #1156
Newark, DE 19711
www.speedypublishing.com
Copyright 2017

All Rights reserved. No part of this book may be reproduced or used in any way or form or by any means whether electronic or mechanical, this means that you cannot record or photocopy any material ideas or tips that are provided in this book.

Part of the United States Constitution is the Bill of Rights, ten statements about the rights of individuals. What does the Bill of Rights say, and how did it get into the Constitution? Let's find out.

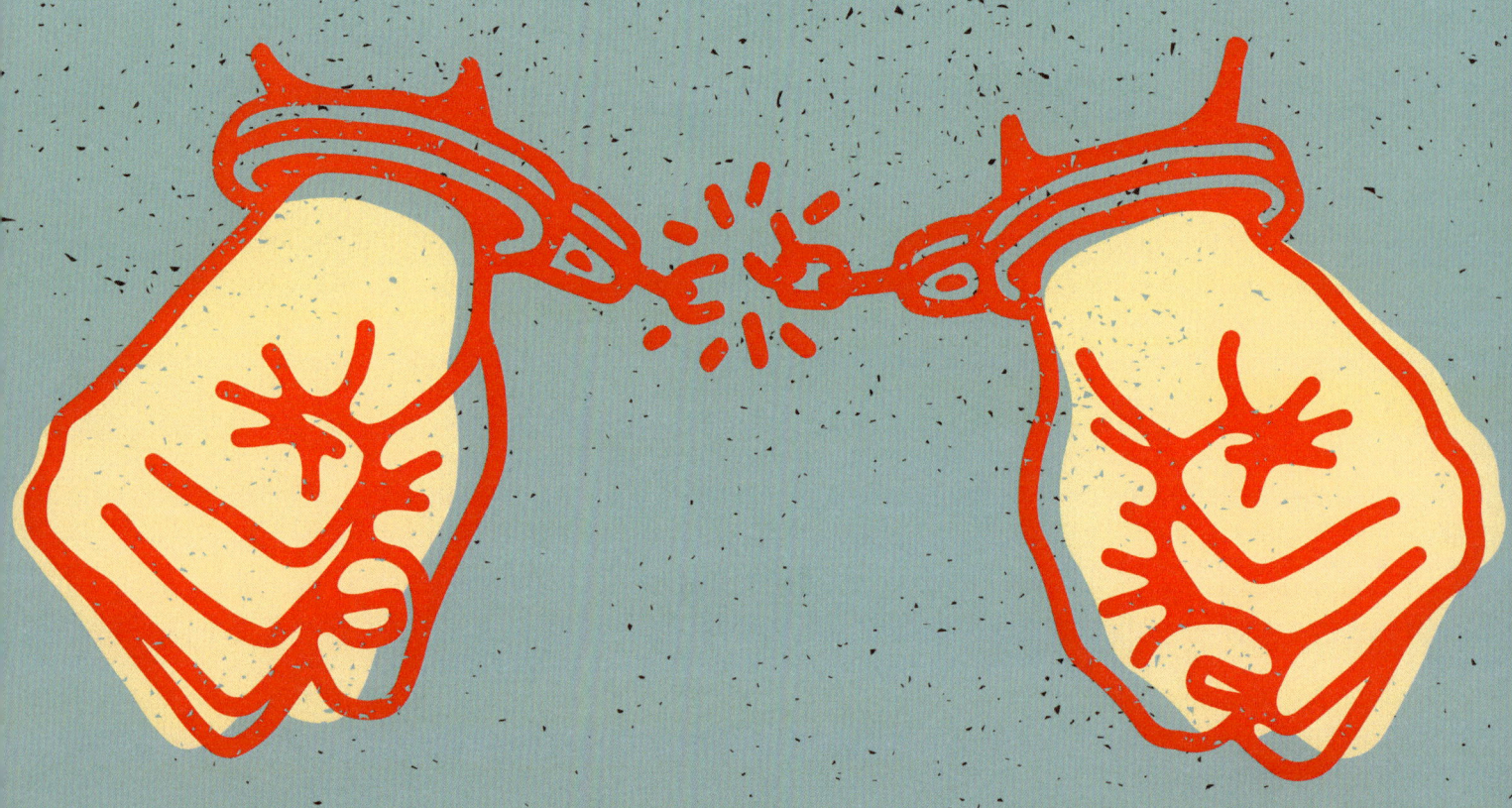

FREEDOM FROM SLAVERY

THE SOUL OF THE CONSTITUTION

As delegates were writing the new Constitution for the United States in the summer of 1787, there were several tense discussions. Some delegates wanted laws that would eliminate slavery, while delegates from slave-holding states demanded the right to continue that practice.

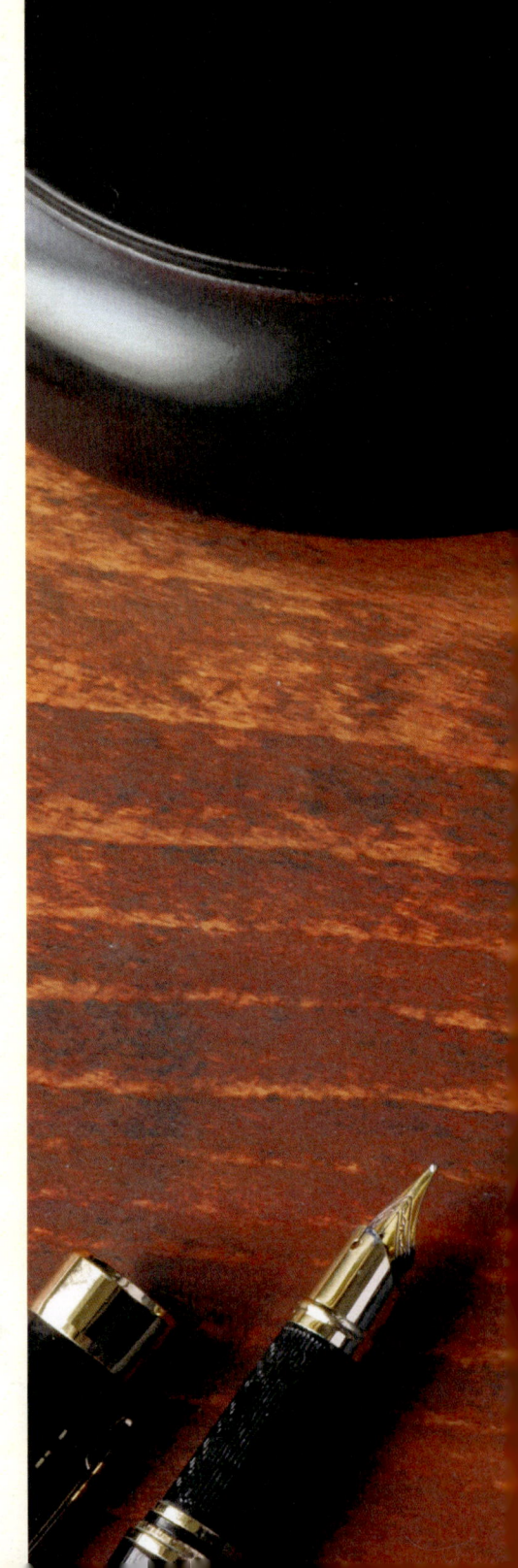

Large states wanted more power for large states, while small states wanted each state to have the same amount of power in the central government, no matter how large it was.

But one of the biggest complaints was that, while the Constitution set up the structure of the federal government, and listed the powers of its various offices, it didn't list anywhere the rights and powers of individuals.

Most of the delegates agreed that the rights of the individuals needed to be included, but wanted more time to put together a good list of those rights. So a deal was struck: the delegates would approve the Constitution without the addition of the rights of individuals, and those rights would be added as amendments as soon as the texts were available.

The Constitution was approved in 1787 and ratified (two-thirds of the states approved it) in 1788. Twelve amendments, mainly dealing with individual rights, were approved by Congress in 1789. The states ratified ten of them by 1791, and they became part of the Constitution.

Scene at the Signing of the Constitution of the United States

KING JOHN SIGNING THE MAGNA CARTA

CREATING THE BILL OF RIGHTS

As the committee started to create the amendments about the rights of individuals, they had a lot of material to help them!

They drew on rights that had been established in documents going back more than five hundred years, like England's Magna Carta.

The 1225 version of the Magna Carta, for example, establishes the right of people to be tried in front of a judge and jury, and the Bill of Rights copies that right.

One strong influence was the English Bill of Rights of 1689, that includes a number of phrases that the amendments in the Constitution copied. For instance, both documents say that individuals have the right not to experience "cruel and unusual punishments", such as torture.

CRUEL PUNISHMENT

THE FRENCH REVOLUTION

A third key document was Virginia's Declaration of Rights, which was written in 1776, just before the start of the American Revolution. This document had a huge influence on reformers in Europe as well as North America, and was an inspiration for the French Declaration of the Rights of Man at the start of the French Revolution. Read more about that in the Baby Professor book The French Revolution: People Power in Action.

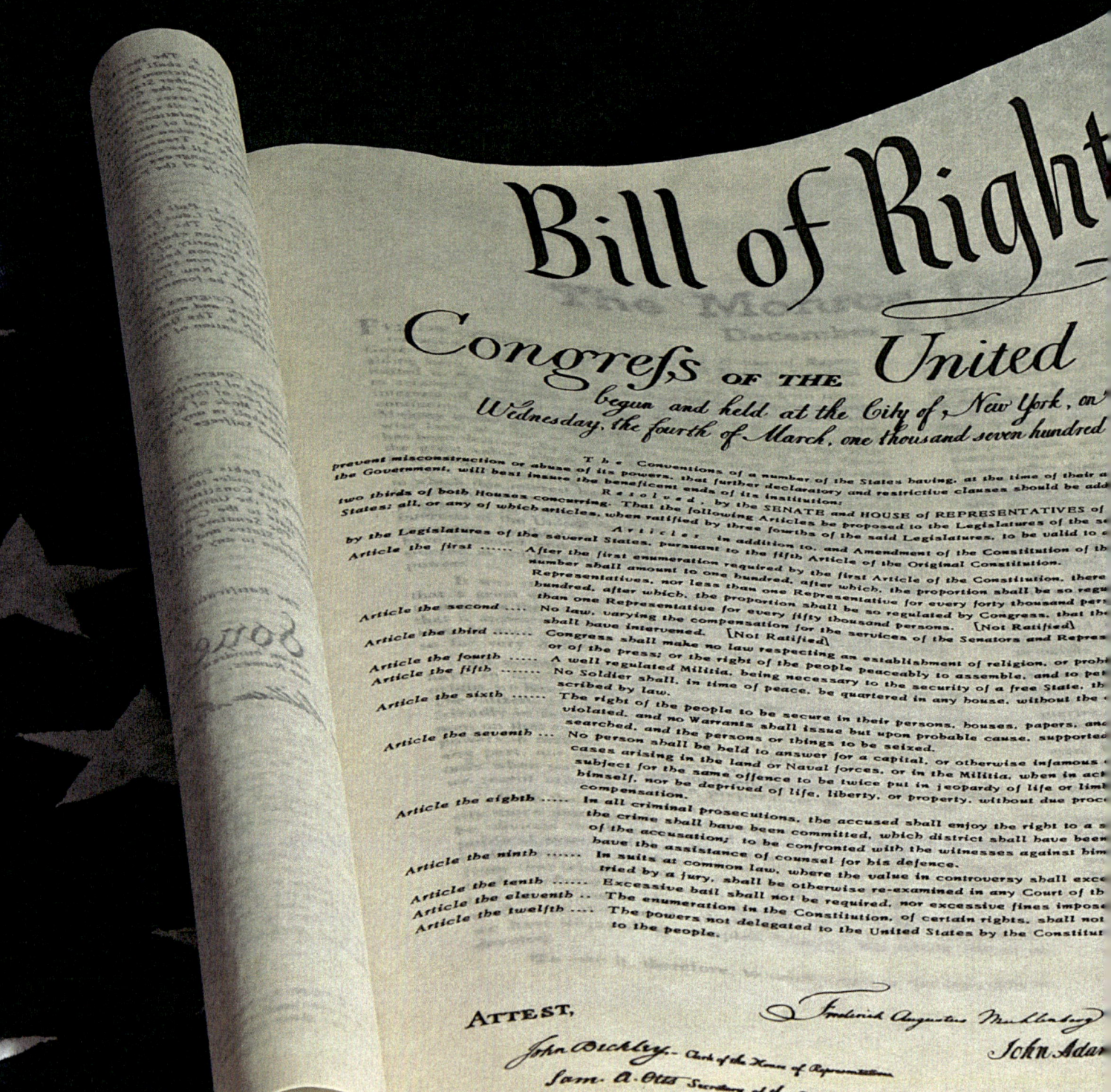

WHAT THE BILL OF RIGHTS SAYS

The ten amendments to the Constitution that we know as the Bill of Rights put at the center of United States law certain "natural rights" that all people hold in common, whether they are rich or poor, homeowners or homeless.

1. The First Amendment says that all people have four freedoms: they are free to say what they want, publish what they want, get together freely with other people, and organize protests when they are unhappy about something.

2. The Second Amendment says that, because it is important for the states to be able to organize their defense, people have the right to "bear arms", that is, own weapons like pistols and rifles.

SOLDIERS

3. The Third Amendment says that the army cannot take over your house and force you to let soldiers sleep in your beds and eat your food, when there is not a war or emergency, without your permission. If there is an emergency, the army can only do that with orders from the government.

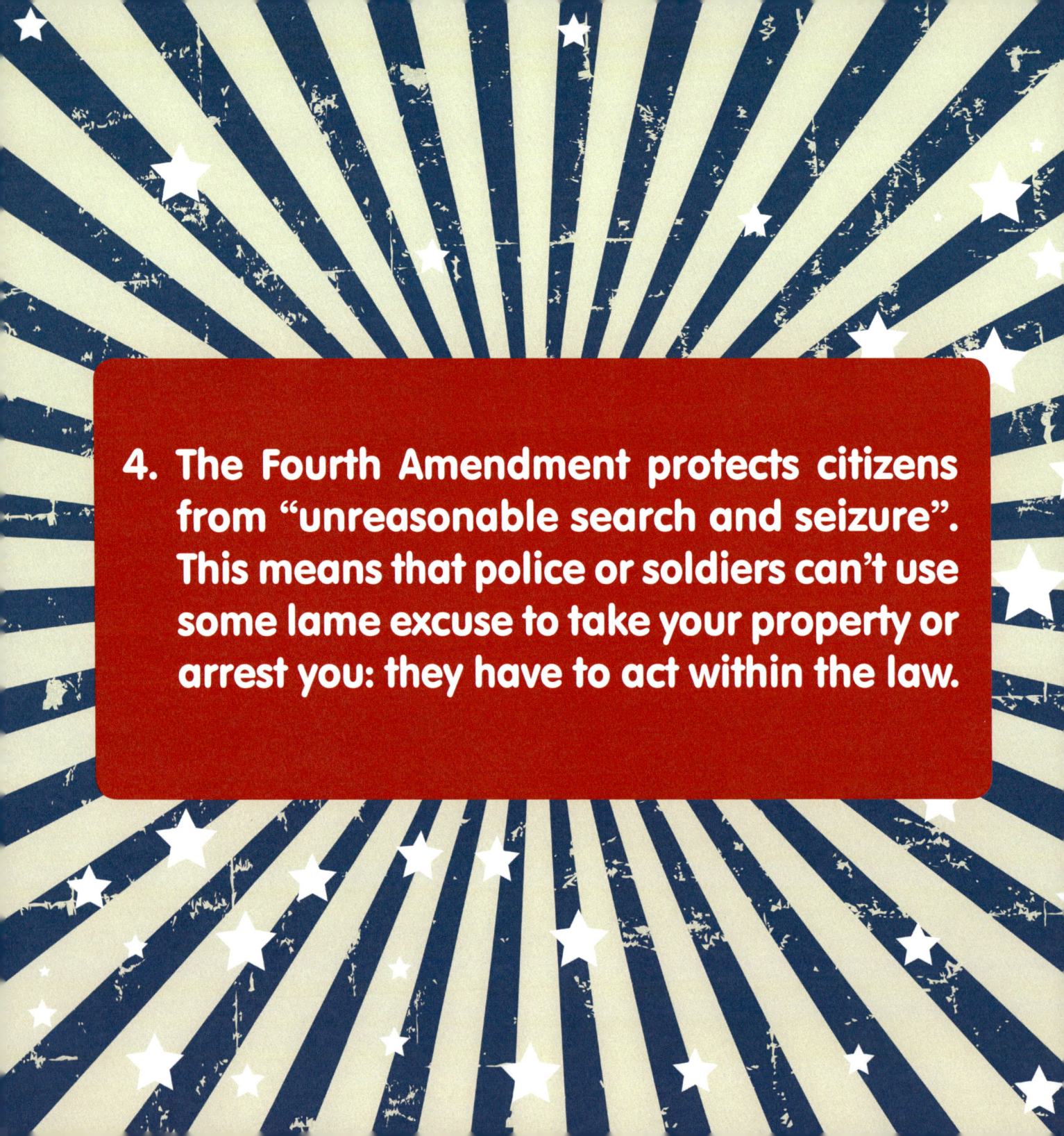

4. The Fourth Amendment protects citizens from "unreasonable search and seizure". This means that police or soldiers can't use some lame excuse to take your property or arrest you: they have to act within the law.

A POLICE OFFICER ARRESTING YOUNG MAN

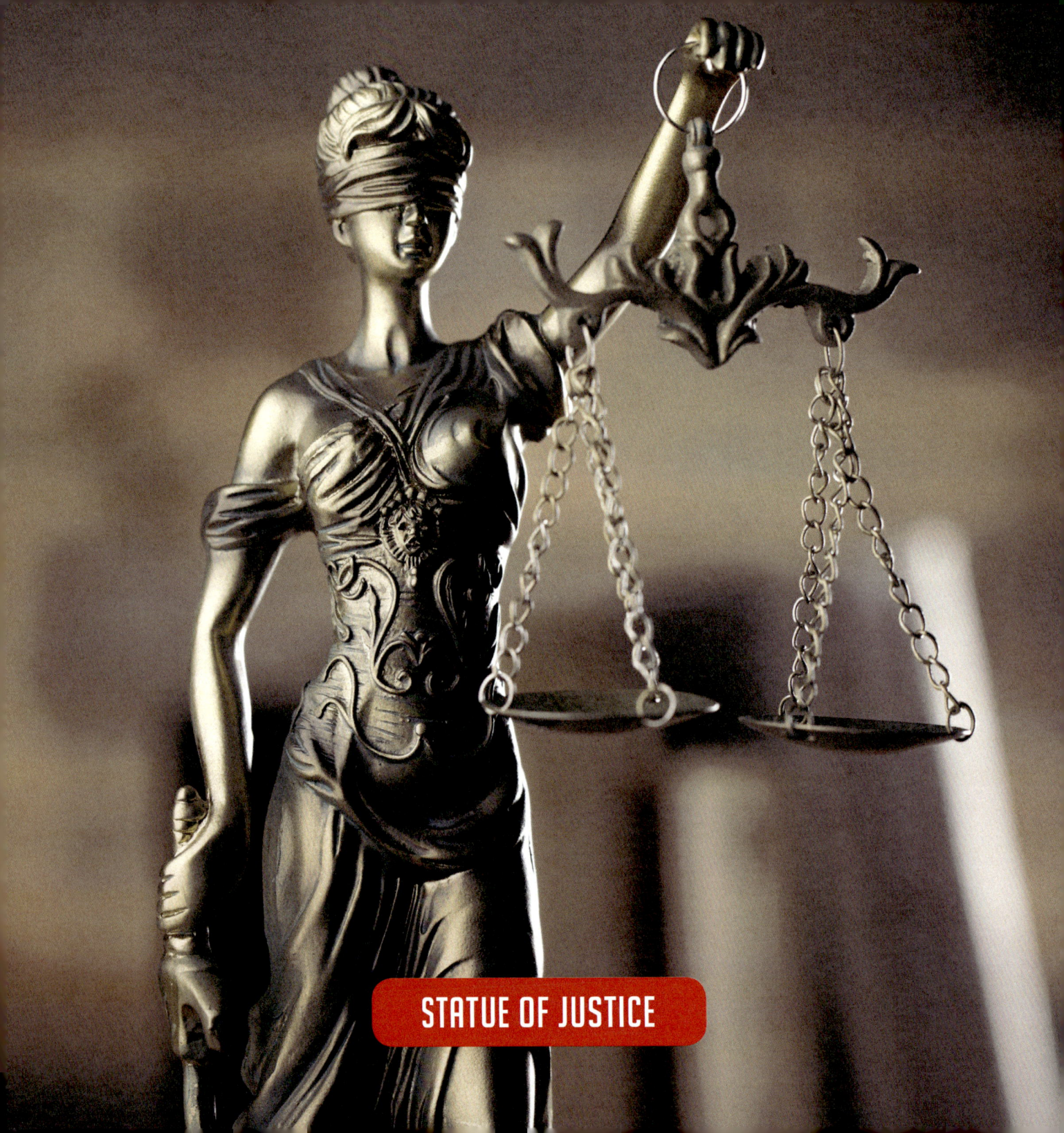

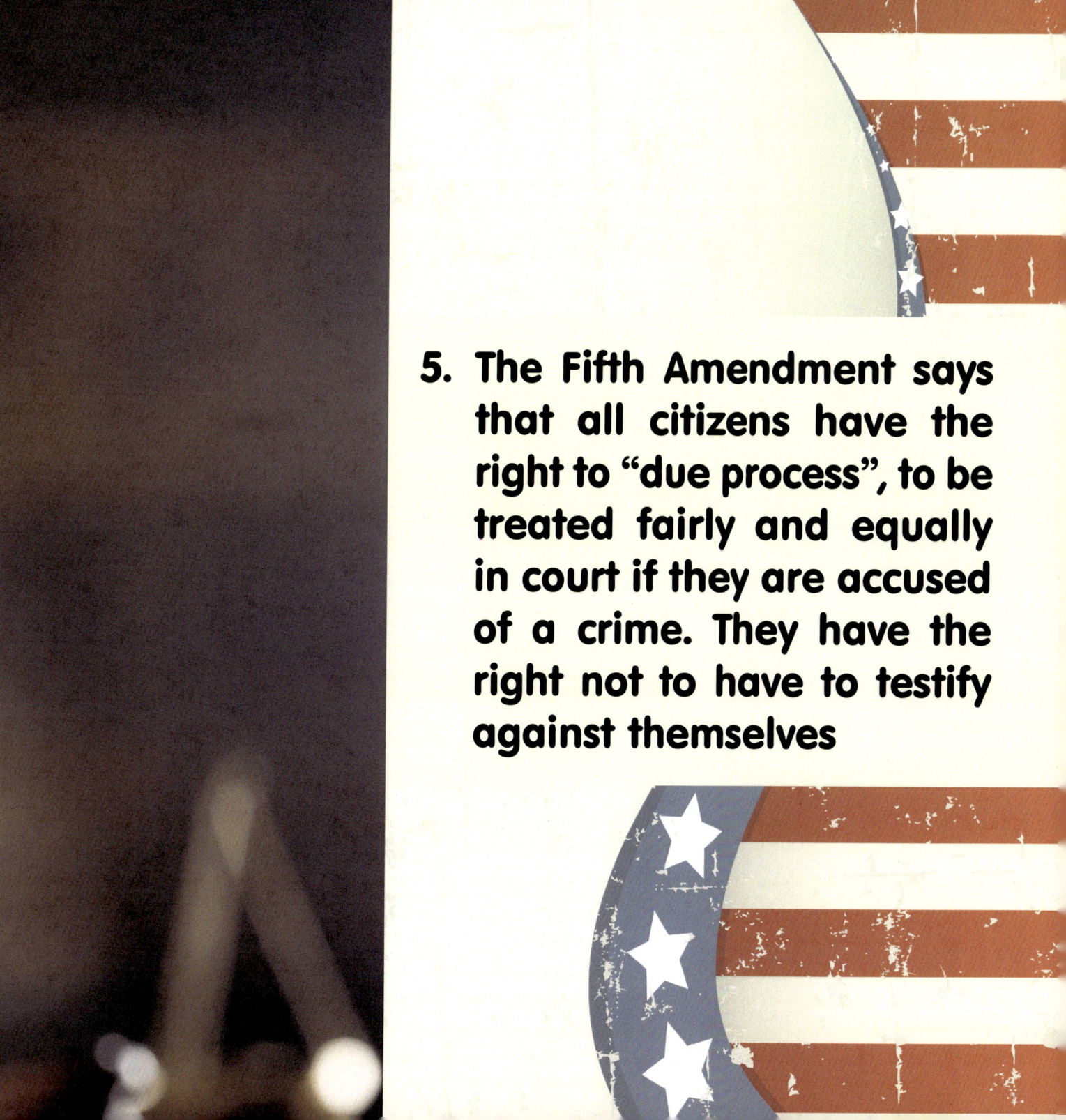

5. The Fifth Amendment says that all citizens have the right to "due process", to be treated fairly and equally in court if they are accused of a crime. They have the right not to have to testify against themselves

6. The Sixth Amendment extends the rights to "due process", so that citizens have the right to not have to wait a long time between when they are charged with something and when they go on trial, and they have the right to trial in front of a judge and jury, and the right to have an attorney helping them.

7. The Seventh Amendment says that people involved in civil disputes (this person says that person owes him money) also have the right to a trial in front of a jury.

8. The Eighth Amendment protects citizens from being tortured, or from other "cruel and unusual punishment", and from being held under conditions that don't match the charge they are facing.

9. The Ninth Amendment basically says that naming certain rights in the Constitution doesn't mean citizens don't have other rights, or that those rights are less important. This is a clause to try to make sure that the Bill of Rights doesn't accidentally make things worse, instead of better, for someone.

10. The Tenth Amendment says that the states have all rights and powers that are not specifically listed for the federal government.

It is worth noting that, when these amendments were written and became part of the United States Constitution, they only applied to white men! Women and people of color had much more limited rights. It was only over a long period of time, education, and struggle, that the country accepted the idea that rights are rights for all people, no matter whether they are male or female and no matter what the color of their skin or their place of origin is.

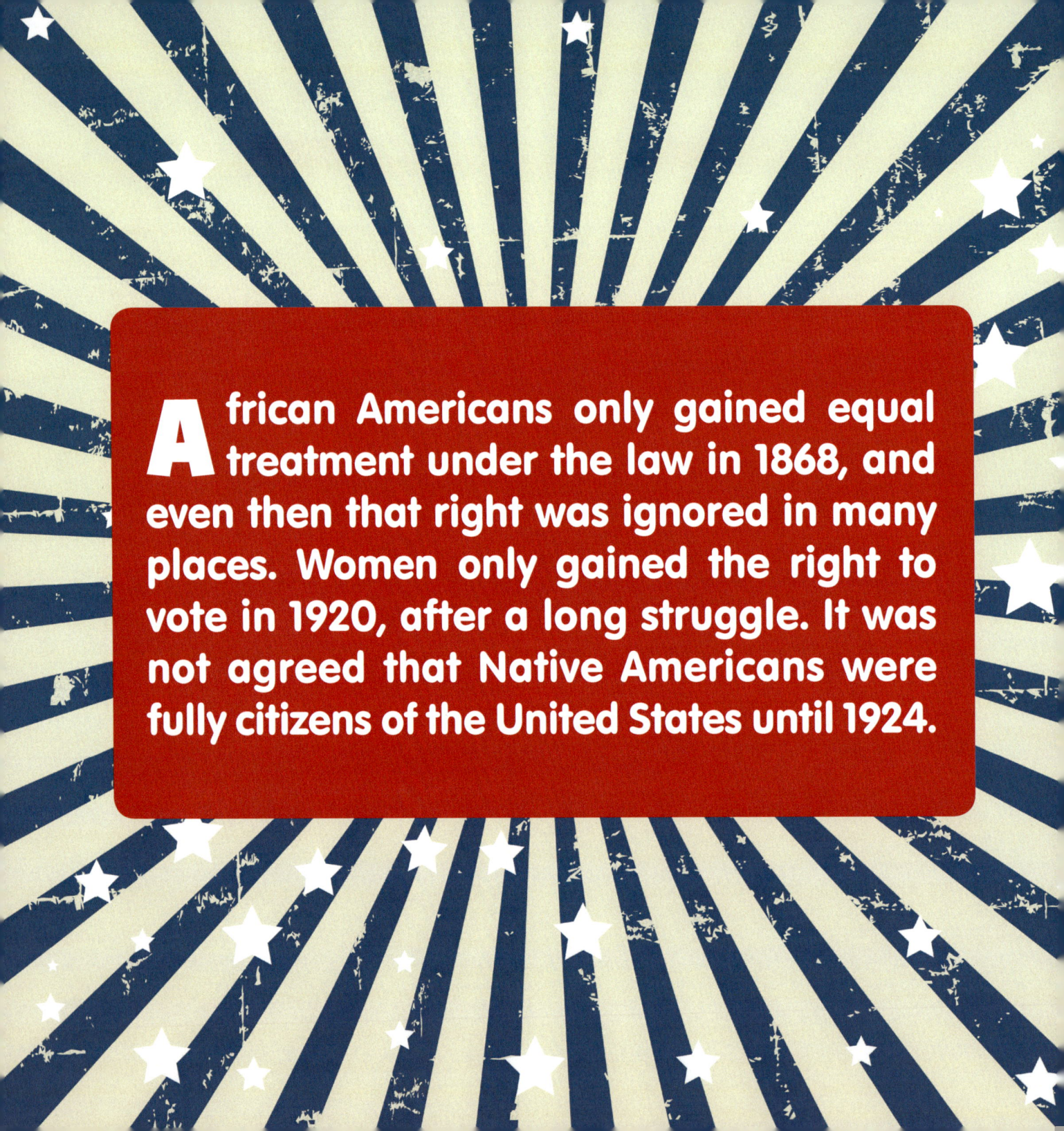

African Americans only gained equal treatment under the law in 1868, and even then that right was ignored in many places. Women only gained the right to vote in 1920, after a long struggle. It was not agreed that Native Americans were fully citizens of the United States until 1924.

BILL OF RIGHTS FUN FACTS

Here are some interesting facts about the Bill of Rights.

★ The committee that wrote the amendments submitted seventeen to Congress. Congress approved twelve of them and sent them to the states to be ratified (approved). A constitutional amendment requires approval by two-thirds of the states, and only ten of the amendments got that approval.

However, an eleventh amendment, about when raises for members of congress can take effect, stayed "pending" for almost two hundred years. It was finally ratified, and became the Twenty-Seventh Amendment to the Constitution, in 1992!

★ When the Bill of Rights was approved, President Washington had one handwritten copy made for the federal government, and one for each of the states. Twelve of the copies still exist.

GEORGE WASHINGTON

★ **December 15th each year is Bill of Rights Day, a good time to celebrate the rights we all share.**

★ It only take two-thirds of the states ratifying an amendment for it to become part of the Constitution. Massachusetts, Georgia, and Connecticut didn't get around to formally ratifying the Bill of Rights until 1939, when the amendments had been part of the Constitution for about 150 years.

THE UNITED STATES

★ Until the twentieth century, the Bill of Rights did not have much impact on the laws of the United States. Since 1900, though, the ten amendments have been cited often in decisions about whether a law is constitutional and people have to obey it, or is unconstitutional so that people can ignore it. In a famous series of cases in the 1960s, when people burned United States flags to show they disapproved of certain government actions, state governments passed laws saying that flag-burning was illegal. The Supreme Court overruled those laws in 1989, saying that what the people were doing was exercising their First Amendment rights to free expression and to protest.

★ **In courtroom dramas you often hear witnesses "take the fifth". They are saying that, under the Fifth Amendment, they do not have to give information that might lead to them being found guilty of something.**

SOLDIERS ON A MARCH

★ The amendment you almost never hear about is the Third Amendment. Preventing the army from taking over your house or barn and putting soldiers in it was very important to the writers of the Bill of Rights, because that is something the British Army did during the American Revolution. There has been little need to call on this constitutional right in the United States in recent times.

The Bill of Rights exists to make sure that governments do not forget that citizens have rights, and that those rights don't depend on the government. Those rights exist naturally, just because people are people. The Bill of Rights is part of the United States Constitution and helps to keep a balance between government power and the power and rights of individuals.

THE LIVING CONSTITUTION

The United States is governed by its Constitution, a document that sets how the government works, what powers the individual states have and—perhaps most importantly—what rights each individual has. Read more about the Constitution, how it came to be, and how it has evolved, in the Baby Professor book C is for Constitution.

Made in the USA
Lexington, KY
28 July 2018